HOW TO TEACH AMERICAN LITERATURE

Student Review Questions and Tests

Elizabeth McCallum Marlow

WestBow
PRESS®
A DIVISION OF THOMAS NELSON
& ZONDERVAN

WestBow Press books may be ordered through booksellers or by contacting:

WestBow Press
A Division of Thomas Nelson & Zondervan
1663 Liberty Drive
Bloomington, IN 47403
www.westbowpress.com
1 (866) 928-1240

ISBN: 978-1-9736-1405-0 (sc)
ISBN: 978-1-9736-1404-3 (e)

Print information available on the last page.

WestBow Press rev. date: 02/15/2018

To the Teacher

The following review questions and tests are designed to be used in conjunction with *How to Teach American Literature: A Practical Teaching Guide*. All review questions and tests are included in the teaching guide and reproduced in this booklet with answers omitted.

Review questions

Copy and distribute a set of review questions to your class. Students break into small groups and refer to their literature books and notes as each group discusses the questions. Every student answers the questions in his or her notebook. On an assigned day, students hand in their notebooks with the completed questions for grading. At a later date, the teacher should review with the class appropriate answers to each set of review questions. The teacher may choose to use some of the questions on tests and semester exams.

Tests

Test procedure[1]

A. Taking tests[2]
Have students clear their desks and take out a pen. Distribute tests. Require students to place a cover sheet on top of their tests and move it down to cover answers as they take the test. The teacher may also wish to arrange the desks at some distance apart. Instruct students to use the back of the test if they require more space for their responses. As students finish a test, they should place it face down on their desks and work on other assignments until everyone has completed the test. Collect the tests.

B. Reviewing tests
Distribute graded tests and review answers. While grading the tests, the teacher may opt to note down excellent responses and ask individual students to read those responses to the class. Take time to answer students' questions about both questions and responses.

---

[1] I have found the following procedures to be effective. Other teachers may prefer to adopt methods that are more suited to the needs of a particular class.

[2] Some tests require the teacher to copy certain excerpts or poems and attach them to the back of the test.

Literature holds up a mirror to life and in so doing allows us to better understand ourselves and others.

Contents

Review questions on Puritan writers

Name _____

1. The Puritans adopted a "plain style" of writing. Define what is meant by this style. Then explain why Puritan writers adopted this writing style.

2. Why do you think Bradford included the incident concerning the death of a "profane young man" in his historical account?

3. Mention one example from Bradford's book of the Puritans' selflessness.

4. Why was Rowlandson's *Narrative of Her Captivity* popular in England?

5. Explain why Bradford's writing is objective whereas Rowlandson's *Narrative* is a subjective piece of writing.

6. Why is Sarah Kemble Knight's *Journal* invaluable to historians?

7. Define Edwards's three metaphors in his "Sinners" sermon and explain why they are effective for his purpose.

8. How does Edwards end this sermon?

9–10: Briefly explain how the following works illustrate the writer's ability to endure affliction because he or she trusted in the Lord:

9. Rowlandson's *A Narrative of Her Captivity*

10. Bradstreet's poetry

11. Refer to "The Author to Her Book." Explain why John Woodbridge referred to Bradstreet as "the tenth muse."

12. Explain why Bradstreet refers to her poetry as the "ill-formed offspring of my feeble brain."

13. Based on facts you have learned about Bradstreet's personal life, why is it extraordinary that she was able to write a large body of poetry?

14. In what sense does the tone of Sarah Kemble Knight's *Journal* differ radically from other Puritan literature you have read?

Review questions on Enlightenment writers

Name _____

1–8: Identify Patrick Henry and Thomas Paine's rhetorical strategies in each passage below. Choose from the following list. You may need to use some terms more than once, and you may decide that a particular quotation illustrates two rhetorical strategies:

allusion, metaphor, anticipating and refuting objections, analogy, emotional appeal, rhetorical question, *ad hominem*

PATRICK HENRY:

1. I have but one lamp by which my feet are guided and that is the lamp of experience.

2. Suffer not yourselves to be betrayed with a kiss.

3. I know not what course others make take, but as for me, give me liberty or give me death.

4. They tell us, sir, that we are weak, but when shall we be stronger?

THOMAS PAINE:

5. Servile, slavish, self-interested fear is the foundation of Toryism.

6. If a thief breaks into my house, burns and destroys my property, and kills or threatens to kill me, or those that are in it, and to "bind me in all cases whatsoever" to his absolute will, am I to suffer it?

7. Let it be told to the future world that in the depth of winter, when nothing but hope and virtue could survive, that the city and the country alarmed at one common danger, came forth to meet and to repulse it.

8. The summer soldier and the sunshine patriot will, in this crisis, shrink from the service of their country.

9. List four of Franklin's non-literary achievements.

10. Benjamin Franklin is an American icon. With reference to his *Autobiography*, explain why for the last two hundred years Americans have so much admired him.

11. Explain Franklin's plan for personal growth. Then point out the plan's main deficiency.

12. Based on some of the sayings found in *Poor Richard's Almanack*, what seems to have been Franklin's opinion of human nature?

13. State the historical context of Patrick Henry's famous speech and explain its result.

14. Explain how Thomas Paine's ideas expressed in the excerpt we read from *The Age of Reason* attack fundamental doctrines of Christianity.

15. In Phillis Wheatley's poem addressed to George Washington, the poet makes frequent use of personification in order to create sympathy for the American cause. Provide examples of this device.

16. Wheatley strongly implies that God is on America's side. Provide examples of this implication.

Review questions on Bryant, Longfellow, Whittier, Holmes, Lowell, and Poe's poetry

Name _____

1. List and define three devices Bryant uses that make "Thanatopsis" a formal poem.

2. Explain why the two poets' attitudes to death in "Thanatopsis" and "Do Not Go Gentle into That Good Night" differ significantly. Mention the author of the second poem.

3. *Snow-Bound* is a pastoral poem. Define that term.

4. Drawing on several sections of Whittier's poem, summarize the picture it depicts of life for a nineteenth-century rural family.

5. Mention one or two family members and others included in the poem who tell stories and summarize the stories they told.

6. Summarize what you learned about the school teacher mentioned in Whittier's poem.

7. Identify the social problem that is explored in "Maud Muller." Explain why this would not be a significant problem in contemporary America.

8. What is Longfellow's main concern in his sonnet "Mezzo Cammin"? Write out the English translation of the title.

9. What analogy does Longfellow use in his sonnet "Divina Commedia"?

10. Another sonnet Longfellow wrote is titled "Nature." What is the main topic of this poem? Explain why it is a typically Romantic poem.

11. Identify and explain the effectiveness of the main poetic device Longfellow uses in "Ship of State."

12. Identify the poet's tone in "Old Ironsides." State the concern the poem deals with. List and explicate several literary devices Holmes uses to convey that concern.

13. Identify the predominant tone in *A Fable for Critics*. Briefly summarize Lowell's opinion of three of the following nineteenth-century poets: Bryant, Hawthorne, Emerson, Poe, Lowell himself.

14. What is Lowell's main concern in the excerpts we read from his poem "The Present Crisis"? What important lesson have you derived from studying the poem?

15–17: Reread the following lines from "The Present Crisis" and explain their meaning:

15. Truth forever on the scaffold, Wrong forever on the throne.

16. Was the Mayflower launched by cowards, steered by men behind their time?
    Turn those tracks toward Past or Future, that made Plymouth Rock sublime?

17. Launch our Mayflower, and steer boldly through the desperate winter sea,
    Nor attempt the Future's portal with the Past's blood-rusted key.

18. Summarize the varying moods of the speaker in Poe's "The Raven."

Review questions on Henry David Thoreau

Name _____

You should refer to *Walden* and *The Night Thoreau Spent in Jail*
as you answer the following questions.

Questions 2–10 refer to *Walden*.

1. Explain why Thoreau is the quintessential non-conformist.

2. What wisdom did you find in *Walden* that you can apply to your own life?

3. What does Thoreau mean when he says he wants "to live deep and suck out all the marrow of life"?

4. What does he mean by these words: "keep your accounts on your thumbnail"?

5. Explain the point of Thoreau's reference to railroads.

6. What do you infer about Thoreau's attitude to his beans? What comparisons does Thoreau make when he describes pulling weeds in his bean field?

7. Summarize the loon episode. What is the point of the episode?

8. Apart from growing beans, pulling weeds, and chasing a loon, how else does Thoreau occupy his time at Walden Pond?

9. Why does he eventually leave Walden Pond?

10. How would Thoreau react to the lives of most contemporary Americans?

11. Refer to the play we read, *The Night Thoreau Spent in Jail*. Explain why Thoreau went to jail. What was Thoreau's response to his aunt's action?

12. List some events in Thoreau's personal life that the playwrights include in the play. In your response, you should include references to Thoreau, his brother, Ellen Sewell, Emerson, Ball, and Bailey.

13. To what extent did *The Night Thoreau Spent in Jail* help you understand this odd man?

Review questions on *The Scarlet Letter*

Name _____

1. Define the novel's setting.

2. Explain why this is a carefully constructed novel.

3. What moral does the rosebush outside the jail appear to symbolize?

4. In addition to the rosebush, mention one or two other instances of Hawthorne's renowned ambiguity in this novel.

5. What does Hawthorne appear to most dislike about seventeenth-century Puritans?

6. Explain the inaccurate impression that most Americans have gained about our Puritan ancestors based on this novel.

7. In addition to Roger Chillingworth's deformity, by what other means does Hawthorne suggest that Hester's husband is demonic?

8. To what extent is Hester's husband to blame for the tragic events?

9. When Hester and Pearl arrive at the Governor's mansion, why does Hawthorne mention the child's reflection in a convex mirror?

10. Throughout most of the novel, Pearl usually acts as a symbolic character rather than a realistic child. When does she cease to be merely a symbol?

11. Apart from the rosebush and Pearl, mention several of the novel's other symbols.

12. In addition to appearing on the scaffold, what other acts does the minister perform to vainly atone for his sin?

13. What is the importance of the forest scene?

14. Explain the townspeople's change in attitude to Hester.

15. List one or two differences between Hester's and Dimmesdale's standing on the scaffold—Hester at the beginning and Dimmesdale in the middle of the book. What is the significance of these differences?

16. During the second scaffold scene, three people react to the minister's cry. Give their names and the significance of all three people.

17. Explain how Hawthorne makes Hester a sympathetic character.

18. In your opinion, who is the greater sinner, the minister or the husband? Explain your opinion.

19. In your opinion, who is the novel's protagonist? Defend your opinion.

20. After Dimmesdale's death, what happens to Chillingworth, Hester, and Pearl?

21. Mention some historical people that Hawthorne includes in the book. Explain what he gains by including them in the story.

22. Although this may not be the most enjoyable book you have ever read, it has remained popular throughout the centuries since its publication. List several reasons for its enduring reputation.

Review questions on Whitman and Dickinson's poetry

Name _____

1. In what way is the poem entitled "I Hear America Singing" a celebratory poem?

2. Do you sympathize with the speaker in Whitman's poem "When I heard the learn'd astronomer"? Why or why not?

3. Referring in detail to one of Whitman's poems about Abraham Lincoln, discuss the poet's attitude to the President's death.

4. What is the major difference between biblical connotations of the word "grass" and Whitman's use of the word in his poem "Song of Myself"?

5. What biographical facts about Dickinson help to explain her detachment from others?

6. Mention some stylistic oddities that make her poems unconventional.

7. Much of Dickinson's poetry is heavily ironic. Explain the irony in the poem that begins "I'm nobody! Who are you?"

8. Dickinson was preoccupied, often morbidly, with the subject of death and writes about the topic in many of her poems. Choose one poem and explain how it conveys her attitude to death. Identify the poem by its first line.

9. Dickinson was a religious skeptic. Based on one poem, evaluate her approach to the Christian faith. Identify the poem by its first line.

10. Dickinson is a Regional writer; she claimed she saw "New Englandly." Referring to two of her poems, demonstrate her ability to minutely describe the natural world. Identify the poem by its first line.

11. Refer to the poem that begins "Success is counted sweetest" and identify Dickinson's central point.

12. List several differences between the poetry of Walt Whitman and Emily Dickinson.

Review questions on *Adventures of Huckleberry Finn*

Name _____

1. List several examples of Twain's satiric attack on Romantic fiction.

2. Identify two incidents that convey Twain's attack on Southern aristocrats.

3. Referring to Pap's diatribe against the government, explain the reason for Pap's misplaced anger.

4. How does Huck escape from his brutal father?

5. Summarize the agonizing mental conflict that Huck struggles with for most of the novel. Give both sides of his dilemma.

6. How does Huck eventually resolve his dilemma?

7. What is the essential difference between Huck and Tom's personalities?

8. Give two specific examples of Tom's activities, one at the beginning and one at the end of the novel.

9. At one point during their time together, Huck and Jim discuss the wisdom of Solomon. Explain Jim's opinion about this biblical character. What is the point of this conversation?

10–15: Clearly identify these people:

Sherburn, Emmeline Grangerford, Boggs, the Duke of Bridgewater, Harney Shepherdson, Miss Watson

16. Defend the truth of the following statement: White men in *Huckleberry Finn* are often immoral and black men are often men of integrity.

Review questions on Bierce, Jewett, London, and Crane's fiction

Name _____

1. Identify Sylvia's dilemma in "The White Heron." How is it resolved?

2. Summarize what the story tells us about Sylvia's personality.

3. How does the ornithologist's attitude to nature differ from Sylvia's?

4. Why is Sylvia's climb up the pine tree so central to the story?

5. What is the grandmother's opinion of Sylvia?

6. Explain how Bierce gains our sympathy for the Confederacy in his story "An Occurrence at Owl Creek Bridge."

7. How does Bierce prejudice us against the Union army?

8. Define the story's setting.

9. How does Bierce manipulate the point of view in this story?

10. Define the setting of London's story "To Build a Fire."

11. Give a valid reason why London chose not to name his protagonist.

12. List aspects of the protagonist's personality that contribute to his death.

13. List several decisions London's protagonist should have made to avoid the tragic outcome.

14. Why does London include the dog in this story of a man's inability to survive?

15. Define the external conflict in "The Open Boat."

16. What is the main internal conflict in this story?

17. List several of this story's symbols and mention their symbolic meaning.

18. Explain what Crane means when he ends the story with these words: "The men on the shore felt that they could then be interpreters."

19. Explain why "The Bride Comes to Yellow Sky" satirizes Western fiction. In your response, deal with the following four elements: the marshal, the villain, the saloon, and the shoot-out.

20. Briefly identify Henry Fleming's attitudes to the tall soldier's death and the tattered soldier's curiosity about his wound in *The Red Badge of Courage*.

21. Explain the irony involved in Henry's "red badge of courage."

22. Mention one or more aspects of Henry's character that create in you a certain affinity for him.

23. Summarize Henry's feelings at the end of *The Red Badge of Courage*.

Review questions on *The Great Gatsby*

Name _____

1. What is the significance of the oculist's sign?

2–6: Briefly identify the main character traits of the following characters:
   Tom Buchanan, George Wilson, Jordan Baker, Meyer Wolfshiem, Myrtle

7. How does Gatsby reinvent himself?

8. Who are Klipspringer and Owl Eyes?

9. What is Jordan Baker's function in this novel?

10. Who is Dan Cody?

11. What is the difference between the people who live in East Egg and those who live in West Egg?

12. What is the Valley of Ashes, and why is it significant in this novel?

13. Why does Nick come to New York, and why does he return to the Midwest at the end of the novel?

14. Identify and explain the technique the author uses at the end of the novel.

15. What is the reason for Gatsby's parties, and why do they end?

16. Provide some reasons why this novel is considered a masterpiece.

Review questions on *The Old Man and the Sea*

Name _____

1. Explain the story's central conflict.

2. Why doesn't Hemingway allow Manolin to sail with Santiago out to sea?

3. Why does Hemingway allow the sharks to eat the marlin?

4. Why does Santiago constantly dream about DiMaggio, arm wrestling, and lions?

5. Explain the function of the tourists at the end of novel.

6. Give several examples of the ways in which Hemingway depicts the old man as a Christ figure.

7. Suggest a theme for this novel.

8. What is your opinion of this theme?

9. Santiago is said to exemplify the Hemingway code of hero. In your opinion, is this old man a hero? Why or why not?

10. In a few sentences, define Hemingway's legendary writing style.

Review questions on Frost's poetry

Name _____

1. Explain how the allusions in "Nothing Gold Can Stay" contribute to the poem's theme.

2. The poem "Design" appears to argue that a sinister design governs this universe. Explain how a reader of this poem comes to this conclusion.

3. "Mending Wall" explores a fundamental difference of opinion between two New Englanders. Define the conflict.

4. Do you agree with the attitude of the speaker or the neighbor in "Mending Wall"? Explain your opinion.

5. Explain how Frost uses a natural scene in "Birches" as a backdrop against which he explores a universal need.

6. Identify the conflict in this poem.

7. Think about "Acquainted with the Night" and name some of the connotations of "night"?

8. What added meaning does the clock supply?

9. How do the details in "Bereft" contribute to the mood of the poem?

10. Discuss the difference in the husband and wife's attitudes to Silas' return in "The Death of the Hired Man."

11. Identify the difference in Warren and Mary's attitudes to one's home.

12. What is your opinion of the ending of "The Death of the Hired Man"?

13. The title of "Once by the Pacific" suggests that as Frost looks out over the turbulent Pacific Ocean, the scene suggests to him a disturbing idea. Identity that idea. What is your reaction to the idea?

Review questions on T. S. Eliot's poetry

Name _____

Questions 1–9 deal with "The Love Song of J. Alfred Prufrock."

1. Summarize J. Alfred Prufrock's personality.

2. What type of neighborhood is Prufrock walking through? How does the setting add to our understanding of Prufrock's personality?

3. Why is it correct to identify this poem as stream-of-consciousness?

4. Why does Prufrock repeatedly refer to women talking about Michelangelo?

5. What details does Prufrock recall about the smart women he thinks about?

6. List three or four items or people to whom Prufrock compares himself. Collectively, what do these comparisons suggest about Prufrock?

7. How does the poem end, and why are these final lines a sad conclusion to Prufrock's introspections?

8. At what moment in the poem does Prufrock feels most alienated from the rest of mankind?

9. This poem manifests the *zeitgeist* or mood of the twentieth century. What mood does Eliot depict throughout the poem?

10. Briefly explain how the excerpts we read from "The Hollow Men" convey a grim picture of modern life.

11. Briefly summarize the content of "Journey of the Magi" in terms of its being an exploration of the poet's conversion experience.

Review questions on *The Glass Menagerie*

Name _____

1. Three of the four main characters in this play want some form of escape. Explicate this statement as it pertains to all three characters.

2. In your opinion, what is the climax of this play?

3. How does the playwright convey the idea that this is a memory play?

4. What are Tom's functions in the play?

5. To what extent, if any, do you sympathize with Tom? Explain your opinion.

6. To what extent, if any, do you sympathize with Laura? Explain your opinion.

7. In spite of Amanda's annoying behavior, the playwright tells us that there is much to admire in her. What can one admire about Amanda?

8. In what ways is Jim "nice" and "ordinary" as the playwright describes him?

9. This is a highly symbolic play. Identify its several symbols.

10. Explain your reaction to the ending.

11. In what sense is Mr. Wingfield a fifth character in the play?

12. Write a paragraph in which you discuss which character you believe to be the play's protagonist.

Review questions on modern and contemporary short fiction

Name _____

1. Provide one or two reasons why O'Connor's story entitled "The Life You Save May Be Your Own" explores the vice of selfishness.

2. Discuss the significance of this story's title.

3. Explain how Tom T. Shiftlet's name reveals his personality.

4. In O'Connor's story "Everything That Rises Must Converge," both Mrs. Chestny and Julian are prejudiced against African Americans. Explain the difference in their attitudes.

5. Apart from their racial bias, what are some other flaws in the personalities of mother and son?

6. Identify the significance of this story's main symbol.

7. Refer to the story "Revelation." Identify and explain the significance of Mrs. Turpin's first revelation.

8. Identify Mrs. Turpin's second revelation.

9. Apply this Bible verse to "Revelation": "But many who are first will be last, and the last first."

10. Summarize the differences between Mrs. May's sons and the Greenleafs' sons in "Greenleaf."

11. Name some defects in Mrs. May's personality.

12. What is your opinion of Mrs. Greenleaf?

13. In terms of its overall meaning, what is your understanding of the ending of "Greenleaf"?

14. Faulkner's "Rose for Emily" is an example of gothic fiction. Explain the term "gothic" and summarize the gothic elements in this story.

15. Explain the clash of two cultures in this bizarre tale. Where does Faulkner stand on the issue?

16. Who is the story's narrator?

17. How do we know that the town's administrators revere the aristocratic Miss Emily?

18. How does Faulkner foreshadow Emily's death? Explain.

19. Does he foreshadow Homer Barron's death? Explain.

20. Referring to Welty's story "A Worn Path," readers have questioned whether or not the grandson was still alive. However, Welty placed emphasis on the journey, the path Phoenix took to get to the clinic. Explain how the path illuminates the story's theme.

21. How do the personalities of minor characters in "A Worn Path" contrast with Phoenix Jackson's character? Mention three minor characters in your response.

22. Why is the contrast between Phoenix and the other characters important to Welty's purpose?

23. What is the central irony of Walter Mitty's life?

24. List the conflicts in Steinbeck's "The Leader of the People."

25. Comment on the grandfather's reaction to Jody's suggestion that they hunt mice.

26. Compare the similarities in the themes of Steinbeck and Thurber's stories.

27. What is the main problem with the couple's marriage in Hemingway's story "Hills Like White Elephants"?

28. Identify and explain the significance of the story's two settings beyond the railroad junction.

29. What is significant about the main setting of this story?

30. Identify the theme of Shirley Jackson's story "The Lottery."

31. Do you agree with Jackson's theme? Explain your opinion.

Review questions on modern and contemporary poetry excluding Frost and Eliot

Name _____

1. It is axiomatic to say that people's circumstances are not always what they seem to be. Explain how E. A. Robinson's poem "Richard Cory" explores the false assumptions we often make about others.

2. Miniver Cheevy realizes he's a failure. Briefly state how he justifies his failure.

3. Briefly summarize Miniver Cheevy's personality.

4. Mention some methods E. E. Cummings uses to convey the joys of childhood in his poem "in Just—"

5. Explain Paul Dunbar's concern conveyed in his poem "We Wear the Mask."

6. In Dunbar's poem addressed to Frederick Douglass, what does the poet wish Douglass could do? For what is Douglass famous?

7. In his poem to Douglass, what metaphor does Dunbar use to refer to America? Briefly comments on the metaphor's effectiveness.

8. What is W. H. Auden satirizing in his poem "The Unknown Citizen"?

9. In what sense is this citizen "unknown"?

10. Refer to Auden's poem "The Shield of Achilles." What does Thetis expect to see on her son's shield?

11. What appears to be the focus of Auden's poem?

12. William Carlos Williams wrote a poem entitled "The Widow's Lament in Springtime." How does the poet convey the depth of the woman's sorrow?

13. Explain how Plath's allusion to the myth of Narcissus enhances the meaning of "Mirror."

14. Refer to Plath's poem entitled "Spinster." Explain how we know that the girl is dissatisfied with her decision to remain a spinster.

15. Think about Langston Hughes's poem "Mother to Son." What advice does the mother give her son?

16. What poetic devices convey the mother's wisdom to the boy?

17. Define the driver's difficult ethical choice in William Stafford's poem "Traveling through the dark."

18. What sort of man is this driver?

19. Explain why he made the right decision.

20. Refer to Elizabeth Bishop's villanelle entitled "One Art." What does the poet accomplish with the switch in perspective?

21. Identify the theme of Countee Cullen's poem "Tableau." How does the poet convey this idea?

22. Briefly summarize the situation described in the poem entitled "When in Rome." Explain why the second speaker's replies are enclosed in parentheses.

23. Explain the attitude of both speakers towards each other.

24. Explain the symbolism of the bicycle lesson in Linda Pastan's poem "To a Daughter Leaving Home."

25. Refer to "Those Winter Sundays." Explain the speaker's change of attitude expressed in Hayden's poem.

26. Why is setting important to E. A. Robinson's poem entitled "The Mill"?

27. We are not explicitly told the course of events in Robinson's poem. Instead, we are left to infer what happens. Summarize the indirection throughout the poem.

28. Explain whether or not the indirection increases the impact of the tragic events on the reader.

29. How does Williams convey his theme in the poem "Landscape with the fall of Icarus"? Why is the poet's use of contrast important?

30. How does Jean Toomer describe a thunderstorm in his poem "Storm Ending"?

Puritan Literature Test

Name _____

- Write detailed, specific answers.
- Do not repeat material used in previous questions.
- Do not repeat the words of the question in your response.

1–5: Identify the author then mention something significant about <u>five</u> of the following six passages:

What would not those poor souls give for one day's opportunity such as you now enjoy. Now you have an extraordinary opportunity, a day wherein —— has thrown the doors of mercy wide open.

Author:

Significance:

They fetched them wood, made them fires, dressed them meat, made their beds, clothed and unclothed them: in a word, did all the homely and necessary offices for them which dainty and queasy stomachs cannot endure to hear named.

Author:

Significance:

I came to Chapter 30, the seven first verses, where I found there was mercy promised again...I do not desire to live to forget this Scripture, and what comfort it was to me.

Author:

Significance:

How dreadful is the state of those that are daily and hourly in the danger of this great wrath and infinite misery! ...If we knew that there was one person, and but one, in the whole congregation that was to be the subject of this misery, what an awful thing would it be to think of!

Author:

Significance:

But here I cannot but stay and make a pause and stand half amazed at this poor people's present condition, and so I think will the reader too when he well considers the same.

Author:

Significance:

[This] caused me to be very circumspect, sitting with my hands fast on each side, my eyes steady not daring so much as to lodge my tongue a hairbreadth more on one side of my mouth than the other.

Author:

Significance:

6. Identify the Puritans' writing style and give a valid reason why they adopted it.

7. Explain at some length why Mary Rowlandson's *Narrative* was popular in England.

8. What was Edwards's purpose in his "Sinners" sermon? Discuss how he uses metaphor to achieve that purpose.

9. Summarize the personality of Sarah Kemble Knight. Provide a major reason why her *Journal* differs from other Puritan writing.

10. What have you learned about seventeenth-century travel from reading excerpts from Madam Knight's *Journal*?

11. Summarize all you have learned about the <u>life and circumstances</u> of Anne Bradstreet.

12. Bradstreet was a devoted mother and grandmother. On the basis of <u>two</u> of her poems and her Meditations, expand on this observation.

13. Summarize the circumstances that compelled Bradstreet to write the poem entitled "The Author to Her Book."

14. Explain in some detail how Bradstreet's religious faith is revealed in her poetry.

Enlightenment Literature Test

Name _____

Benjamin Franklin

1. Discuss what you have learned about Franklin's character from studying his *Autobiography.* In your response, include references to his brother, his journey to Philadelphia, and his plan for moral perfection.

2. Summarize all you have learned about *Poor Richard's Almanack.*

Thomas Paine

The American Crisis, Number 1

3. What does Paine mean by a "summer soldier" and a "sunshine patriot"?

4. Explain what is meant by *ad hominem* rhetoric. At what point or points in the essay does Paine use *ad hominem* attack?

5. Why does Paine include the anecdote about a tavern keeper?

6. When and why did Washington have Paine's essay read to his soldiers?

7. Based on the excerpt you read from Paine's *Age of Reason*, summarize Paine's thoughts about organized religion and the Lord Jesus Christ.

Patrick Henry

8. Henry began his legendary speech by complimenting the patriotism and abilities of the opposition. Why is this strategy effective?

9. Why is it effective that Henry ended his speech with a strong emotional appeal?

10. Why Henry was adamant that compromise was impossible?

11. How did Henry refute the objection that the colonists were unprepared to fight the British?

Phillis Wheatley

12. Summarize all you know about this poet's personal life.

13. Based on your reading several of Wheatley's poems, what is your personal reaction to this poet and her poetry?

Romantic Poetry Test

Name _____

Bryant

"Thanatopsis"

1. In summary form, list three or four consolations the speaker gives a man who is approaching death.

2. What is the speaker's general attitude to death?

Longfellow

"A Psalm of Life"

3. What does Longfellow mean by this imperative: "Tell me not… / Life is but an empty dream!"?

4. According to Longfellow, what can we learn from the lives of great men?

"Divina Commedia"

5. What is this poem's connection to *The Divine Comedy?*

6. In what important way is the poet like the workman Longfellow describes in this poem?

"Nature"

    7.   Explain why "Nature" is a typically Romantic poem.

Whittier

Snow-Bound

    8.   Summarize the boys' chores.

    9.   What does this poem tell us about Whittier's family life?

    10. What happens at the end of the excerpts we read?

"Maud Muller"

    11. Provide a summary of this poem.

    12. What is your opinion of the social problem this poem explores?

Holmes

"Old Ironsides"

    13. Summarize the historical background of this poem. What was the result of the poem's publication?

Lowell

"Fable for Critics"

14. What is Lowell's opinion of his own poetry?

15. Explain whether or not you think his opinions of the following writers are valid: Bryant, Emerson, Hawthorne, and Poe.

"The Present Crisis" [The pertinent stanzas are attached to the back of this test.]

16. Refer to stanza 5 of "The Present Crisis." What decision is the poet alluding to in the first line of this stanza? The stanza includes several contrasts. What overall idea is being contrasted here?

17. Refer to stanzas 15 and 18. What is Lowell implying with his allusions to the *Mayflower* and Plymouth Rock in stanza 15? What is he suggesting in stanza 18?

Poe

"The Raven"

18. In few sentences, summarize the speaker's changing states of mind.

19. Throughout the poem, the speaker's attitude to the raven changes. Name several of these changes. What does the bird finally represent to the speaker? [Do not repeat information supplied in the previous answer.]

20. What is the prevailing mood of the poem?

Whitman and Dickinson Poetry Test

Name _____

Whitman

"When I Heard the Learn'd Astronomer"

1. Explain the Romantic idea this poem conveys.

"I Hear America Singing"

2. What is Whitman's main poetic device throughout the poem? Why is it effective?

"O Captain! My Captain!"

3. Comment on Whitman's poetic devices in this poignant poem written after Abraham Lincoln's assassination.

"When Lilacs Last in the Dooryard Bloom'd"

4. Explain the significance of Whitman's title.

5. Based on your recollection of the poem, how does Whitman recreate the President's funeral? Mention as many details as possible.

Dickinson

6. Summarize all the facts you have learned about Dickinson's life. This question does not require you to discuss her poetry.

7. One poem begins with these lines: "The Soul selects her own Society." What idea does Dickinson explore in this poem?

8. Explain why the content of "This is my letter to the World" makes the poem an appropriate preface to Dickinson's poetry.

9. Explain Dickinson's definition of truth in the poem that begins, "Tell all the Truth but tell it slant—"

10. One of Dickinson's most celebrated poems opens with this line: "I heard a Fly buzz—when I died—" How does the poem mock conventional attitudes to death?

11. How does the poem "The Bustle in a House" appear to convey Dickinson's attitude to death?

12. In one or two sentences, explain Dickinson's meaning in the poem that begins, "'Faith' is a fine invention."

13. Why do you think Emily Dickinson is acclaimed as one of the greatest American poets?

Regional and Naturalist Short Fiction Test

Name _____

"The White Heron"

1. Name the author and state your opinion of the ornithologist.

2. Sylvia is an unusual little girl. Summarize her personality and her circumstances.

3. Explain why we can read Sylvia's climb up the pine tree as a rite of passage.

"An Occurrence at Owl Creek Bridge"

4. Explain how Bierce causes the reader to feel sympathetic towards Farquhar.

5. How does the author cause one to feel hostile to the Union soldiers?

6. Explain why the author's description of the condemned man's final thoughts is a realistic piece of writing.

"To Build a Fire"

7. Summarize your opinion of the protagonist. Based on incidents in the story, support your opinions.

8. If you were in the same circumstances as the protagonist finds himself, what actions would you have taken that differ from his?

9. Why does London include a dog in his story?

"The Open Boat"

10. Why does Crane include a house of refuge and a lighthouse as he describes the men's attempts to get to shore?

11. How does Crane convey his belief in nature's indifference to man's fate?

12. Define the story's main conflict.

"The Bride Comes to Yellow Sky"

13. Crane manipulates the reader's expectations about characters in typical Western stories. How does he depict the marshal and the villain? In your response, provide the names of both characters.

14. In addition to the personalities of the marshal and the villain, what other aspects of Western fiction does Crane satirize?

The Great Gatsby Test

Name _____

1. What is your opinion of Nick Carraway?

2 – 6. Briefly identify these characters:

Dan Cody

Michaelis

Catherine

Meyer Wolfshiem

Mrs. McKee

7. List some details that convey Gatsby's phoniness.

8. List some rumors that circulate about Gatsby.

9. Before Nick meets his neighbor, he sees Gatsby outside his monstrous mansion looking at the stars. Gatsby reaches out toward the green light at the end of the Buchanans' dock. What does this incident symbolize?

10–13: Briefly define these people's personalities:

Tom Buchanan

Myrtle Wilson

George Wilson

Jordan Baker

14. What does the valley of ashes symbolize?

15. What overall impression do you get from the names of people who attend Gatsby's parties?

16. What is the truth about Gatsby's parents?

17. Why do Gatsby's parties end?

18. What does the oculist's sign suggest as it looms over the landscape?

19. Fitzgerald leaves us in no doubt that Daisy loves Gatsby more than she loves her husband, so why doesn't she leave Tom and marry Gatsby?

20. When Fitzgerald mentions a holocaust towards the end of the novel, to what is he referring?

21. Who attends Gatsby's funeral?

22. Did Fitzgerald approve of the lifestyle of Jazz Age socialites? Why or why not?

23. In your opinion, what are some reasons for the enduring popularity of this novel?

Test on the poetry of Robert Frost and T. S. Eliot

Name_____

The poetry you will need to answer questions effectively
is attached to the back of this test.

Robert Frost

"Nothing Gold Can Stay"

1. Write out a one-sentence statement of this poem's theme. Briefly explain how Frost conveys this main idea.

"Birches"

2. In this poem, the poet reflects on his childhood. In what two ways do birch trees become bent over? Which of these two ways of bending birches does Frost prefer and why?

3. The poet's description of birch trees leads him to explore a universal experience. What is that experience?

"Bereft"

4. Although we do not know what or whom the speaker has lost or why he is grieving, Frost provides many details that convey the man's despondency. What are these details?

"Mending Wall"

5. What does the wall in this poem symbolize?

6. What kind of man does the neighbor represent? What is your opinion of the neighbor?

"The Death of the Hired Man"
7. Refer to this poem. Summarize all the poem tells you about Silas, his past and present circumstances.

8. With whose attitude to Silas' return do you sympathize, Mary's or Warren's? Explain your reaction.

"Once by the Pacific"
9. Some of Frost's poetry is very dark. Where is the speaker and what event is forecast in this poem?

10. Briefly explain how Frost conveys this event.

"Acquainted with the Night"
11. How does the poet communicate the speaker's despair?

T. S. Eliot

"The Love Song of J. Alfred Prufrock"
12. Refer to this poem. List several of Eliot's allusions and explain the meaning of several of them.

13. What is the setting of the entire poem?

14. In what sense is it true to say that Prufrock represents Eliot's opinion of modern man?

"The Hollow Men"
15. Refer to this poem. What overall picture of Eliot's contemporaries does this poem convey?

16. How does Eliot convey this impression?

"Journey of the Magi"
17. What is Eliot's purpose in writing this poem? How is that purpose achieved?

Modern and Contemporary Short Fiction Test

Name _____

Support your answers with detailed, appropriate reference to the stories.

"A Rose for Emily"

1. What is the community's attitude to Miss Emily Grierson?

2. Comment on Emily's relationship to the two principal men in her life.

3. Why does Miss Emily go mad?

4. Reread the poem by E. A. Robinson entitled "Richard Cory," which is attached to the back of this test. Explain what Richard Cory has in common with Miss Emily.

"A Worn Path"

5. Summarize the basic difference Welty makes between Phoenix and the people Phoenix encounters during her journey and at the clinic.

6. Write out a one-sentence theme for Welty's story.

7. How does Welty's setting help us to understand the story's central idea?

8. Why does Welty call her protagonist "Phoenix"?

"The Leader of the People"

9. To what extent, if any, do you sympathize with the following characters: Carl Tiflin, the grandfather, Jody? Deal with each person separately.

10. Like all fiction and life itself, Steinbeck's story is full of conflicts. List the various conflicts. Which conflict did you find most interesting? Explain your response.

"The Secret Life of Walter Mitty"

11. Explain why the two main characters in this story are stereotypes.

12. Briefly explain how Thurber uses parody in this story.

"Hills Like White Elephants"

13. Explain the significance of Hemingway's title.

"The Lottery"

14. What main idea is Shirley Jackson attacking in this short story?

15. Mention some ironic details in Jackson's story. What is the overall effect of these details?

"Everything That Rises Must Converge"

16. What is the significance of O'Connor's title? Explain why Mrs. Chestny does not understand what the title clearly states.

17. Why is Julian Chestny more hypocritical than his mother?

18. What traits, good and bad, define Mrs. Chestny's personality?

"Greenleaf"

19. What is the function of the bull that is destroying Mrs. May's property?

20. How does O'Connor clarify the bull's function?

21. In what ways are Mr. Greenleaf's sons different from Mrs. May's boys? Name all four young men. Why are these differences ironic?

"The Life You Save May Be Your Own"

22. Scholars have stated that this story ironically parodies a romance. Defend this reading. In your response deal with the daughter, the tramp, and the setting.

"Revelation"

23. Summarize Mrs. Turpin's personality. How does she change at the end of the story?

24. Why does the college student feel compelled to throw a book at Mrs. Turpin?

General question

25. The clash between dream and reality is said to be at the core of much American fiction. Support this contention with detailed reference to two stories we have read. Do not repeat information supplied in your other responses.

Modern and Contemporary Poetry Test
(excluding Frost and Eliot)

Name_____

(excluding Frost and Eliot)

The poetry you will need to answer questions effectively
is attached to the back of this test.

E. E. Cummings

"anyone lived in a pretty how town"

1. In what way do the lives of "anyone" and "noone" contrast with the lives of other people in their community?

2. Why does the poet refer to the husband and wife as "anyone" and "noone"?

Sylvia Plath

"Mirror"

3. Summarize the myth to which the poet alludes. How does the allusion draw a parallel to the speaker?

William Stafford

"Traveling through the dark"

4. In what sense, apart from the literal meaning, is the speaker "traveling though the dark"?

5. Do you think he makes the right decision? Explain your response.

William Carlos Williams

"Landscape with the Fall of Icarus"
6. How does the poet convey the idea that human beings and the natural world are indifferent to other people's suffering?

"This Is Just to Say"
7. Refer to this poem. Comment on the title. What added information is supplied in the last three lines of this poem?

W. H. Auden

"The Shield of Achilles"
8. Refer to this poem. What is significant about the structure of this poem? How do Hephaestus' carvings defeat Thetis' expectations? What is Auden's main idea?

"The Unknown Citizen"
9. Refer to this poem. What statement does this poem make about the modern world?

10. Do you think the statement can be applied to contemporary America? Explain why or why not.

Langston Hughes

"Mother to Son"

    11. Explain why readers admire this mother.

Paul Dunbar

"Douglass"

    12. Why does the poet appeal to Douglass in this poem?

"We Wear the Mask"

    13. Explain the title of this poem. What is the poet's main concern?

E. A. Robinson

"Miniver Cheevy"

    14. Summarize Miniver Cheevy's personality and his problem.

"Richard Cory"

    15. Define Richard Cory's advantages, and explain the effectiveness of Robinson's surprise ending.

    16. What implicit message does the poem convey?

Robert Hayden

"Those Winter Sundays"
   17. Explain the speaker's change of perspective in this poem.

Elizabeth Bishop

"One Art"
   18. Refer to this poem. Explain how the poet explores the theme of loss in this poem.

Mari Evans

"When in Rome"
   19. Explain in some detail the significance of the title.

Linda Pastan

"To a Daughter Leaving Home"
   20. Explain both the mother and the daughter's attitudes to the daughter's leaving home.

Countee Cullen

"Tableau"
   21. Summarize the situation described in this poem.

Printed in the United States
By Bookmasters